This copy of
'The Land of Utter Nonsense'
belongs to

[illegible] ....

Also in Sparrow by Colin West

Not to be Taken Seriously

[redacted]

THE LAND OF UTTER NONSENSE

Poems Picked & Pictured by

COLIN WEST

SPARROW BOOKS

A Sparrow Book
Published by Arrow Books Limited
17-21 Conway Street, London W1P 6JD

An imprint of the Hutchinson Publishing Group

London Melbourne Sydney Auckland
Johannesburg and agencies throughout
the world

First published by Hutchinson 1983
Sparrow edition 1984

Set in Plantin

Printed and bound in Great Britain by
Anchor Brendon Ltd, Tiptree, Essex

ISBN 0 09 933320 1

Contents

The Sea, *Anon.* 11
The Duck-Billed Platypus, *Michael Flanders* 12
The Heron, *J. B. Morton* 13
Oh To Be, *Mike Griffin* 14
Babies haven't any hair, *Samuel Hoffenstein* 15
On the Bridge, *Anon.* 16
Waste, *Harry Graham* 17
A Pig Tale, *Anon.* 18
A Caution to Hillbilly Singers, Harpists, Harpoonists, Channel-Swimmers, and People first in Line for World Series Tickets, *Ogden Nash* 19
Riddle, *Anon.* 20
A Railway Official of Skewe, *Anon.* 21
The Hippopotamus, *Hilaire Belloc* 22
In Days of Old, *R. A. W. Cox* 24
Little William Arthur White, *Sir Marcus Ordeyne* 26
The Elephant, *John Joy Bell* 27
The Ridiculous Pediculus, *Nicholas Husk* 28

I Don't Suppose, *Anon.* 29
Putting the Shot, *Colin West* 30
The Sword-Fish, *Lord Alfred Douglas* 31
Pray spare a thought for Uncle Joe, *Paddy Roberts* 32
Mohair, *Roger Eckersley* 33
The Three Unlucky Men, *James Reeves* 34
Down behind the dustbin, *Michael Rosen* 36
The Kite, *Michael Braude* 37
Twinkle, twinkle, little star, *Samuel Hoffenstein* 38
The Viking, *Hugh Chesterman* 39
You Must Never Bath in an Irish Stew, *Spike Milligan* 40
If you should meet a Polar bear, *Frank Fear* 41
Henry Sutton, *Anon.* 42
The Sorrows of Werther, *W. M. Thackeray* 43
The Lepidopterist, *Ogden Nash* 44
The Young Maid Who Said Why, *Anon.* 45
We Don't Like that Girl, *Anon.* 45
The Missing Punctuation, *Anon.* 46
The Bard at Bedtime, *Tracey J. Crawford* 47
The Cheerful Crocodile, *T. Bolt* 48
Algy Met a Bear, *Anon.* 50
Hello Jolly Guardsman, *Spike Milligan* 51
The Grunting Gurnard and the Croaking Tench, *Nicholas Husk* 52
Mirror, mirror on the wall, *David Gibbons* 53
Amelia mixed the mustard, *A. E. Housman* 54
My Uncle and Aunt, *Roger Eckersley* 55
A Lesson in Household Pets, *Carolyn Wells* 56
Acid Humour, *Anon.* 58
Tender-Heartedness, *Harry Graham* 59

The Gymnast, *Alistair Sampson* 60
Stay in your Seat, *Matthias Barr* 61
Late last night, *Michael Rosen* 62
Tibetan Lament, *Anon.* 63
Envelope, *D. L. Upton* 64
The Young Man of St Bees, *Anon.* 64
The Art of Good Driving, *Anon.* 65
The Jay, *Michael Braude* 65
Methuselah, *Anon.* 66
Impromptu, *Samuel Wilberforce* 67
There was once a Jill who loved her Jack till,
Alistair Sampson 68
The Square Root, *Carolyn Wells* 69
The Lizard, *Cecil G. Trew* 70
The Headless Gardener, *Ian Serraillier* 71
Lizzie Borden, *Anon.* 72
A Wish, *G. K. Chesterton* 73
Unemployable, *Gareth Owen* 74
Ungulates, *Michael Braude* 75
The violin is something that, *Paddy Roberts* 76
The Darkest and Dingiest Dungeon, *Colin West* 77
Radi, *Anon.* 78
We had a little baby girl, *Herbert R. Allport* 78
Eggs, *Cecil G. Trew* 79
Diplodocus, *Bert L. Taylor* 80
The Old Witch of Malacca, *Walter Parke* 82
Lines to My Wig, *J. P. C.* 83
Tight Squeeze, *Christopher Dearden* 84
Heaven's anger fell on Alfred Ball,
Sir Marcus Ordeyne 85
The Walrus, *Michael Flanders* 86

The Dog's Day, *Anon.* 87
The Man with the Single Hair, *Mel B. Spurr* 88
Wild Flowers, *Peter Newell* 90
Mary had a crocodile, *Sir Marcus Ordeyne* 91
A Wise Old Owl, *Anon.* 92

Index of Poets 93
Acknowledgements 94

THE
LAND OF
UTTER
NONSENSE

The Sea

Behold the wonders of the mighty deep,
Where crabs and lobsters learn to creep,
And little fishes learn to swim,
And clumsy sailors tumble in.

Anon.

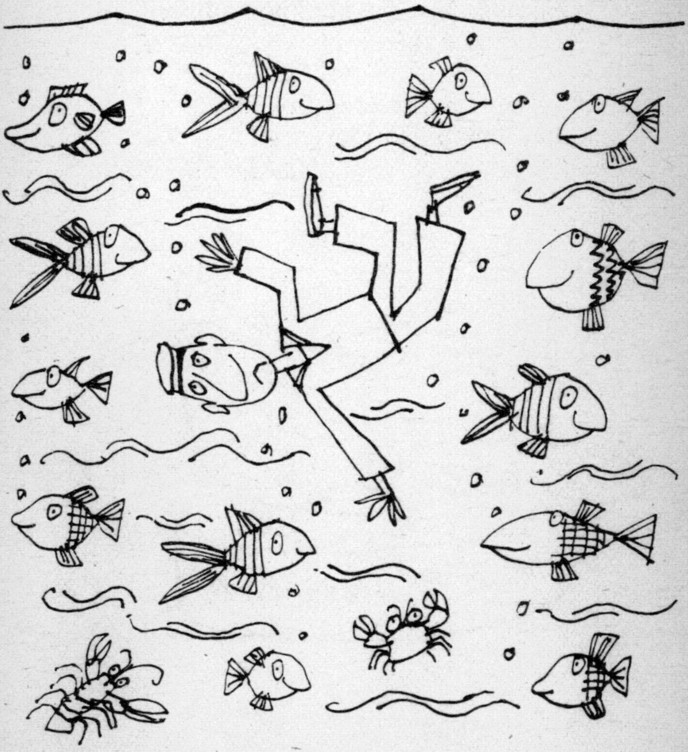

The Duck-Billed Platypus

We call him 'Duck-billed Platypus'
And mock him for his name;
He does not seem to mind it.
He feels no sense of shame
Because he does not know himself
By such a title,
He's
A 'Golden, Shining Love-Bird'
In Duck-billed Platypese.

Michael Flanders

The Heron

A Heron by the river's brim
A simple heron was to Jim,
But if he'd been the little fish
That made that heron's breakfast-dish,
He might have murmured, while being caught,
'Not quite so simple as I thought.'

J. B. Morton

Oh To Be

Oh to be a broken leg
In plaster white as chalk.
And travel everywhere by crutch
While others have to walk.

Mike Griffin

Babies haven't any hair;
Old men's heads are just as bare; –
Between the cradle and the grave
Lies a haircut and a shave.
Samuel Hoffenstein

On the Bridge

He stood on the bridge at midnight,
Disturbing my sweet repose,
For he was a large mosquito –
And the bridge was the bridge of my nose.

Anon.

Waste

I had written to Aunt Maud,
Who was on a trip abroad,
  When I heard she'd died of cramp,
  Just too late to save the stamp.

Harry Graham

A Pig Tale

Two little pigs to market went,
   Their names were Paul and Patience.
They both were sold and both were sent
   To different destinations.

And as the pair were dragged apart
   Paul said in soothing tones:
'Don't cry, we'll meet again, sweetheart;
   I feel it in my bones.'

* * *

They did meet at an early date;
   He had not been mistaken,
Paul was the sausage on my plate
   And Patience was the bacon.

Anon.

A Caution to Hillbilly Singers, Harpists, Harpoonists, Channel-Swimmers, and People first in Line for World Series Tickets

Fame was a claim of Uncle Ed's,
Simply because he had three heads,
Which, if he'd only had a third of,
I think he would never have been heard of.

Ogden Nash

Riddle

He travels so much,
And wherever he goes,
He carries his trunk
At the end of his nose.

Anon.

A Railway Official of Skewe

A railway official of Skewe
Met an engine one day that he knew.
  Though he smiled and he bowed,
  That engine was proud;
It cut him – it cut him in two.

Anon.

The Hippopotamus

I shoot the Hippopotamus
  with bullets made of platinum,

Because if I use leaden ones
his hide is sure to flatten 'em.
Hilaire Belloc

In Days of Old

In days of old
The knights were bold
(Or so we're told).

And every day
Would dragons slay
(Or so they'd say),

And maidens fair
With flowery hair
Save from despair.

And armour clad,
With helm and flag,
Did joust and brag.

But knights today
No longer play
And dragons slay;

And maidens fair
Now take their share
Of toil and care.

Now in this land
The ladies stand
While men do sit
And sometimes knit;

'Tis plain to see
That chivalry
Is not to be.

R. A. W. Cox (13)

Little William Arthur White
Found a keg of dynamite.
His parents are now picking small
Bits of Willie off the wall.

Sir Marcus Ordeyne

The Elephant

Aunt Mary is my aunt,
  She took me to the Zoo.
She offered to the Elephant
  One bun – it wanted two.

Aunt Mary had a hat
  All cherries on her head.
The beast thought, 'Buns are good,
  But that will do quite well instead.'

The creature smiled serene,
  And made a little bow . . .
Aunt Mary's never, never seen
  Her hat from then till now.

Aunt Mary danced a jig,
  And wept till she was blind,
And screamed, 'You bad, old ugly pig!'
  But, it didn't seem to mind.

John Joy Bell

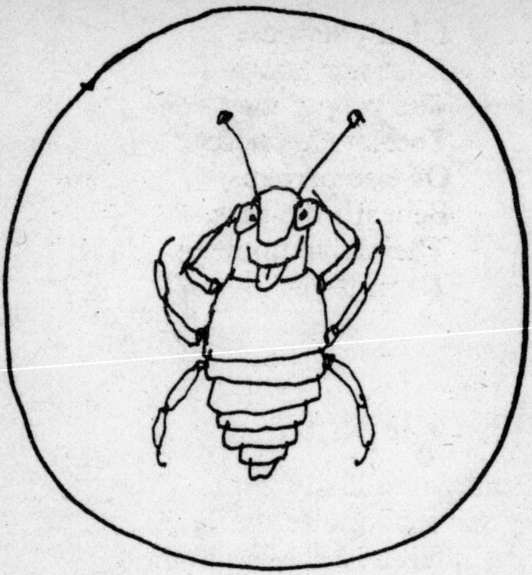

The Ridiculous Pediculus

What name is more ridiculous
Than Apterus pediculus?
   Why treat with such respect
   This squalid small insect?
   Let's rather disinfect
Our scrubbed and cleanly person
Which nothing could be worse on –
   Let alone about the house:
Pediculus? Ridiculous!
   Let's be frank – the Common Louse.

Nicholas Husk

I Don't Suppose

I don't suppose
A lobster knows
The proper way
To blow his nose,
Or else perhaps
Beneath the seas,
They have no need
To sniff and sneeze.

Anon.

Putting the Shot

Tomorrow I may put the shot,
Or on the other hand, may not;
For yesterday I put the shot,
But where I put it, I forgot.

Colin West

The Sword-Fish

The Sword-fish is an awful brute,
He tears your hair out by the root.

And when you're bathing in the sea,
He leaps upon you suddenly.

And if you get out on the sand,
He sometimes follows you inland.

Lord Alfred Douglas

Pray spare a thought for Uncle Joe,
Who used to blow the piccolo.
One night he tried to play on it
A rather tricky twiddly bit:
It didn't quite work out somehow,
For something made him sneeze, and now
The piccolo's in Uncle Joe
And he's in such a pickle-O.

Paddy Roberts

Mohair
(The hair of an Angora goat)

Said the Angora goat
On a defensive note:
'It's better to have mohair
Than no hair.'

Roger Eckersley

The Three Unlucky Men

Near Wookey Hole in days gone by
   Lived three unlucky men.
The first fell down a Treacle Mine
   And never stirred again.

The second had no better fate
   And he too is no more.
He fell into a Custard Lake
   And could not get to shore.

The third poor fellow, sad to say,
  He had no fairer luck,
For he climbed up a Porridge Hill
  And halfway down got stuck.

Alas, alas! man is but grass,
  Let life be short or long;
And all the birds cried 'Fancy that!'
  To hear this merry song.

James Reeves

Down behind the dustbin
I met a dog called Sid.
He could smell a bone inside
but couldn't lift the lid.

Michael Rosen

The Kite

Short of temper is the kite,
always spoiling for a fight,
and what will seldom mollify one
is telling it to go and fly one.

Michael Braude

Twinkle, twinkle, little star,
But stay, my darling, where you are;
Into my life if you should fall,
I'd never see you shine at all.

Samuel Hoffenstein

The Viking

The Viking whom you see in books
Was justly noted for his looks;
A six-foot-two of blood and bone
Who turned the scale at fourteen stone.
He passed his lifetime making trips
In highly decorative ships,
But airs and graces had he none,
He did the things that are not done.
Regarded as a gentleman
I fear he was an 'also ran'.

Hugh Chesterman

You Must Never Bath in an Irish Stew

You must never bath in an Irish Stew
It's a most illogical thing to do.
  But should you persist against my reasoning
  Don't fail to add the appropriate seasoning.

Spike Milligan

If you should meet a Polar bear,
please take this advice:
just hop and jump about a bit –
it helps to break the ice.

Frank Fear

Henry Sutton

Henry Sutton
Made his wife
Serve him mutton
All his life.

When going to sleep,
His mind was rested
By counting the sheep
That he'd digested.

Anon.

The Sorrows of Werther

Werther had a love for Charlotte
  Such as words could never utter;
Would you know how first he met her?
  She was cutting bread and butter.

Charlotte was a married lady,
  And a moral man was Werther,
And for all the wealth of Indies,
  Would do nothing for to hurt her.

So he sigh'd and pined and ogled,
  And his passion boil'd and bubbled,
Till he blew his silly brains out,
  And no more was by it troubled.

Charlotte, having seen his body
  Borne before her on a shutter,
Like a well-conducted person,
  Went on cutting bread and butter.

W. M. Thackeray

The Lepidopterist

The lepidopterist with happy cries
Devotes his days to hunting butterflies.
The leopard, through some feline mental twist,
Would rather hunt a lepidopterist.
That's why I never adopted lepidoptery;
I do not wish to live in jeopardoptery.

Ogden Nash

The Young Maid Who Said Why

There was a young maid who said, 'Why
Can't I look in my ear with my eye?
  If I give my mind to it,
  I'm sure I can do it,
You never can tell till you try.'

Anon.

We Don't Like that Girl

We don't like that girl
From Tooting Bec,
She washes her face,
And forgets her neck.

Anon.

The Missing Punctuation

Caesar entered on his head
A helmet on each foot
A sandal in his hand he had
His trusty sword to boot

Anon.

The Bard at Bedtime

Shakespeare said,
'I'll go to bed,
'Tis nearing the end of day;
But first I'll wash my socks out
And then I'll write a play.'

Tracey J. Crawford

The Cheerful Crocodile

Upon the sacred river Nile
There lives a lazy long reptile
Who's full of greed and full of guile,
Whose skin's as rough as any file,
Who's got a wide deceptive smile
That's visible at half a mile;
Of course you've guessed that, all the while,
I'm speaking of the crocodile.

Perhaps you do not like his style –
His manners, I admit, are vile,
But glum folk – those who never smile –
Might with advantage pause awhile
And ponder on the crocodile.

Observe – he can digest a file
Or armour-plated projectile.
But he prefers a nice fragile
Young duckling, or an infantile
Fat calf: he cannot reconcile
Himself to beasts that are senile;
He likes them plump and juvenile.

Now does he chase his prey a mile?
Not he! he just lies still awhile,
Like some old log or wooden pile
That's stranded in the river Nile.
Then ducklings that are infantile
And calves, all plump and juvenile
In droves, without one thought of guile
Down his expansive throat defile;
All lured on by that wide wide smile.

Now this riparian reptile
Is sinful, and I hate his style,
But still, glum folk, just think awhile.
You're wise, I know, and versatile,
Yet times will come when life seems vile,
When good things miss you by a mile,
When troubles come in one big pile,
And things occur you feel would rile
A saint. But scowling's so futile,
So don't. Think of the crocodile,
Then, like him, just sit still awhile, and smile.

T. Bolt

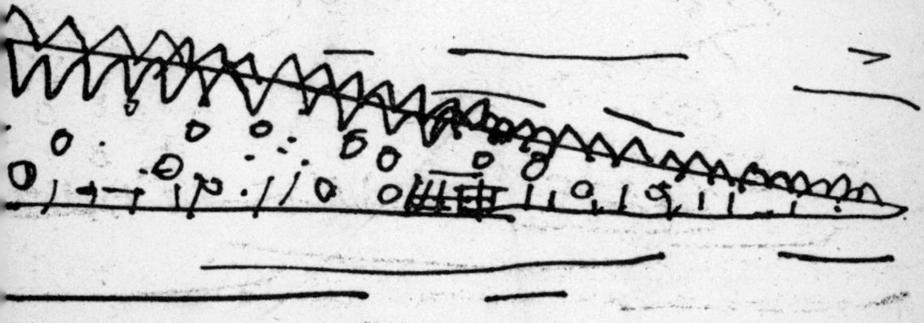

Algy Met a Bear

Algy met a bear,
A bear met Algy.
The bear was bulgy,
The bulge was Algy.

Anon.

Hello Jolly Guardsman

‘Hello Jolly Guardsman
In your scarlet coat:
It reaches from below your tum
To halfway up your throat.

‘Tell me jolly Guardsman
When you’re off parade
What kind of clothes do you put on?’
‘Civvies I’m afraid.’

Spike Milligan

The Grunting Gurnard and the Croaking Tench

I fish, but never have I found
My victims utter any sound:
This voicelessness some folk refute,
Denying fish are always mute.
'Tis said that gurnards grunt like hogs
   And herrings squeak like mice;
I've read that tench can croak like frogs –
   Are audible through ice . . .
The self-same book denies with glee
A claim that dolphins bark like dogs –
I must aver I do prefer
   A silent sea.

Nicholas Husk

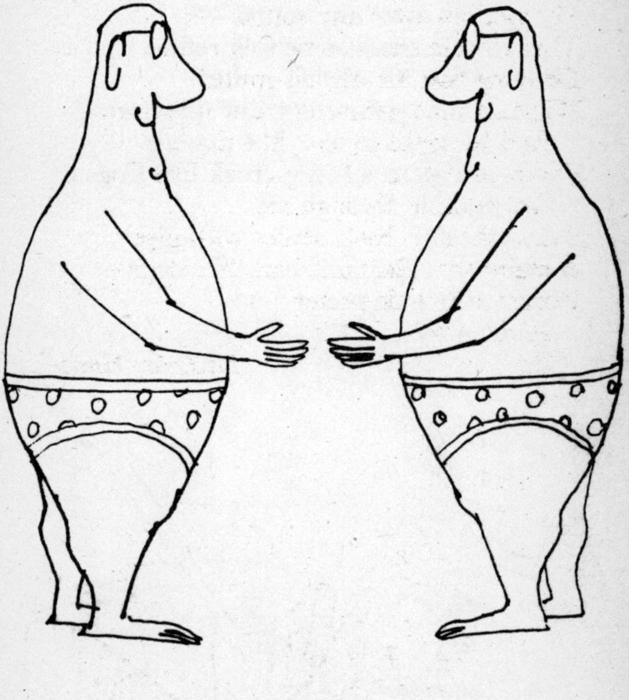

Mirror, mirror on the wall,
You make me fairest one of all,
For though my looks are not renowned,
They're not so bad the wrong way round.
David Gibbons

Amelia mixed the mustard,
  She mixed it good and thick;
She put it in the custard
  And made her mother sick,
And showing satisfaction
  By many a loud huzza
'Observe' said she 'the action
  Of mustard on Mamma.'

A. E. Housman

My Uncle and Aunt

My uncle lives with my aunt in Persia;
He keeps two cows and one is an Ayreshire;
He wants to be happy but somehow can't –
Though he loves his cows he hates my aunt.

Roger Eckersley

A Lesson in Household Pets

Dear Child, who wants a household pet,
  For you these lines are written.
Don't let your Aunt or Mother get
  A bird, or dog, or kitten,
But tell them, for a pleasant change
  From those old hackneyed creatures,
You'd like a beast of wider range
  And less familiar features.

For nature's lessons can't be learned
  In schoolroom or in college;
But by proximity discerned
  Is perfect nature knowledge.
So do not tramp the wild, wet wood,
  And get all damp and muddy;
But in your nursery, sweet and good,
  Pursue your nature study.

So, Child, whatever be your age,
  Instead of a Canary,
Just keep within your gilded cage
  A pretty Dromedary.
'Twill teach you more of nature-lore
  Than wearisome researches,
To hear the little darling roar,
  And hop about on perches.

A few nice Jaguars will give
  A lot more fun than rabbits;
Then you can notice how they live
  And study their queer habits.

And I'm prepared to guarantee,
  If you like life and action,
Two Jaguars, or maybe three,
  Will give you satisfaction.

When you by day are playing round,
  Or when at night you're sleeping,
A pet Rhinoceros, I've found
  Will well repay the keeping.
By day he'll willingly be fed
  With all the folks provide you;
At night, upon your little bed,
  He'll cuddle down beside you.

Of course it may not seem to you
  I've mentioned very many,
But I have just picked out a few
  Which I think best of any.
If you make Aunt or Mother get
  All these I've recommended,
Your poor old-fashioned household pet
  Will find its reign is ended.

Carolyn Wells

Acid Humour

Poor old Brown is dead and gone
His face you'll see no more,
For what he thought was H_2O
Was H_2SO_4.

Anon.

Tender-Heartedness

Billy, in one of his nice new sashes,
Fell in the fire and was burnt to ashes;
Now, although the room grows chilly,
I haven't the heart to poke poor Billy.

Harry Graham

The Gymnast

Willie was proud of his handstand.
He did it on the local grandstand,
He did it on the bandstand
And he did it on the sands and
He did it so much in the sun
That his feet got overdone
But he never got his hands tanned.

Alistair Sampson

Stay in your Seat

Have you forgotten the road to your mouth,
Whether it lies in the north or the south?
Feeding your eyes and your nose with your dinner
Won't make you fatter, but very much thinner.
Besides, who would kiss such a queer-looking boy?
Mamma won't behold you with feelings of joy.
Next time you are given your dinner to eat,
Please do it more cleanly, and stay in your seat.

Matthias Barr

Late last night
I lay in bed
driving buses
in my head.
Michael Rosen

Tibetan Lament

The loveliest of our lamas
Is gone beyond the door.
He'll never wear pyjamas
Any more, any more.

Above the yawning chasm
He tried to pass a yak;
It took a sneezing spasm
And blew him off his track.
Now the silent valley has him,
And he can't come back.

The loveliest of our lamas
Is gone beyond the door.
He'll never wear pyjamas
Any more.

Anon.

Envelope

The sky is an envelope
The world is a letter
And I am a full stop
That knows no better

D. L. Upton

The Young Man of St Bees

There was a young man of St Bees
Who was stung on the arm by a wasp;
  When they said, 'Does it hurt?'
  He replied, 'No it doesn't:
It's a good job it wasn't a hornet.'

Anon.

The Art of Good Driving

The art of good driving's a paradox quite,
Though custom has proved it so long;
If you go to the left, you're sure to go right,
If you go to the right, you go wrong.

Anon.

The Jay

Its colours are not bright or gay,
nor is its song surpassing sweet:
what most distinguishes the jay
is how it walks across a street.

Michael Braude

Methuselah

Methuselah ate what he found on his plate,
And never, as people do now,
Did he note the amount of the calory count:
He ate it because it was chow.
He wasn't disturbed as at dinner he sat,
Devouring a roast or a pie,
To think it was lacking in granular fat
Or a couple of vitamins shy.
He cheerfully chewed each species of food,
Unmindful of troubles or fears
Lest his health might be hurt
By some fancy dessert;
And he lived over nine hundred years.

Anon.

Impromptu

If I were a cassowary
   On the plains of Timbuctoo,
I would eat a missionary,
   Cassock, bands and hymn book too.
Samuel Wilberforce

There was once a Jill who loved her Jack till
She fell head over heels for a Pterodactyl
This went on as a matter of fact till
She found out he was too utterly prehistoric for words.

Alistair Sampson

The Square Root

The Square Root is not nice a bit.
   Mathematicians dig for it;
They seem to relish it, but I
   Think it exceeding hard and dry.
Yet 'tis of use, for I suppose
   From it a branch of learning grows.

Carolyn Wells

The Lizard

The Lizard, catching insects small,
His stomach fortifies.
I keep one in the dining room
To save me swatting flies.

Cecil G. Trew

The Headless Gardener

A gardener, Tobias Baird,
sent his head to be repaired;
he thought, as nothing much was wrong,
he wouldn't be without it long.

Ten years he's weeded path and plot,
a headless gardener, God wot,
always hoping (hope is vain)
to see his noddle back again.

Don't pity him for his distress –
he never sent up his address.

Ian Serraillier

Lizzie Borden

Lizzie Borden with an axe,
Hit her father forty whacks.
When she saw what she had done,
She hit her mother forty-one.

Anon.

A Wish

I wish I were a Girl Guide,
And looked so bright and neat
And made my young subordinates
Salute me in the street.
But none have ever called me neat
And few have thought me bright
And the young who see me are amused
And double up at sight.

I wish I were a Girl Guide,
And wore so large a hat
Curled up abruptly at the side
With a nice cockade like that.
My hat is large but shabby
And without that cock or curl
Few would mistake me for a guide
Or even for a girl.

G. K. Chesterton

Unemployable

'I usth thu workth in the thircusth,'
He said,
Between the intermittent showers that
emerged from his mouth.
'Oh,' I said, 'what did you do?'
'I usth thu catcth bulleth in my theeth.'

Gareth Owen

Ungulates

When ungulates arrange to mate,
the ungulates are never late,
and when they tryst they do not tarry
but go ahead at once and marry:
all this might well explain why horses
will hardly ever seek divorces.

Michael Braude

The violin is something that
Is strung with guts of pussy-cat:
And listening to it, sometimes I've
A feeling that the cat's alive.
P.S. to play the violin
You really need a double chin.

Paddy Roberts

The Darkest and Dingiest Dungeon

Down in the darkest and dingiest dungeon,
Far from the tiniest twinkle of stars,
Far from the whiff of a wonderful luncheon,
Far from the murmur of motoring cars,
Far from the habits of rabbits and weasels,
Far from the merits of ferrets and stoats,
Far from the danger of mumps or of measels,
Far from the fashions of fabulous coats,
Far from the turn of a screw in a socket,
Far from the fresh frozen food in the fridge,
Far from the fluff in my dufflecoat pocket,
Far from the bite of a mischievous midge,
Far from the hole in my humble umbrella,
Far from my hat as it hangs in the hall,
I sit here alone with myself in the cellar,
I *do* so like getting away from it all!

Colin West

Radi

Radi was a circus lion,
Radi was a woman hater.
Radi had a lady trainer,
Radiator.

Anon.

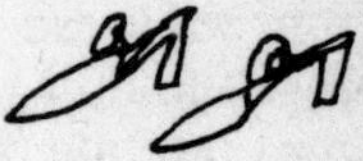

We had a little baby girl
Who made our hearts to flutter.
We used to call her Margarine –
We hadn't any butter.

Herbert R. Allport

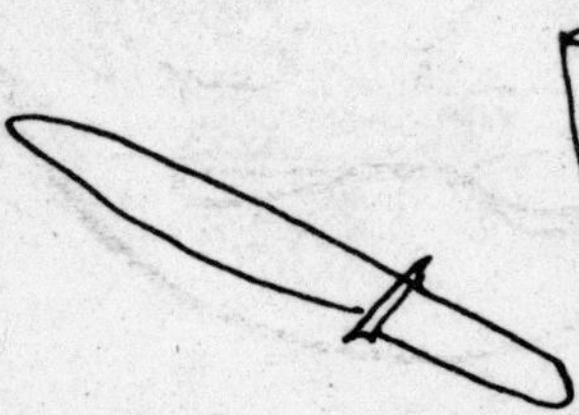

Eggs

All kinds of creatures come from eggs –
Canaries, owls and larks,
And turtles, insects, crocodiles,
And fish and snakes and sharks –
When next at breakfast you should have
Boiled eggs, why then look out!
In opening them be sure that one
Of these does not hop out.

Cecil G. Trew

Diplodocus

Behold the mighty dinosaur,
Famous in prehistoric lore,
Not only for his power and strength
But for his intellectual length.
You will observe from these remains
The creature had two sets of brains –
One in his head (the usual place),
The other at his spinal base.
Thus he could reason *a priori*
As well as *a posteriori.*
No problem bothered him a bit;
He made just head and tail of it.
So wise was he, so wise and solemn,
Each thought filled just a spinal column.

If one brain found the pressure strong,
It passed a few ideas along.
If something slipped his forward mind
'Twas rescued by the one behind.
And if in error he was caught
He had a saving afterthought.
As he thought twice before he spoke
He had no judgement to revoke.
Thus he could think without congestion
Upon both sides of every question.
Oh, gaze upon this model beast,
Defunct ten million years at least.

Bert L. Taylor

The Old Witch of Malacca

There was an old witch of Malacca
Who smoked such atrocious tobacca,
  When tigers came near
  They trembled with fear,
And didn't attempt to attacca.

Walter Parke

Lines to My Wig

My Wig
Is about two sizes too big:
I'm often inclined to think
That, if washed, it might shrink,
But then it might be two sizes too small –
Which would be no use at all.

J. P. C.

Tight Squeeze

A ballerina, named Katrina,
Learned to play the concertina.
Tunes by Bizet
She found easy.
Scheherazade
Proved much harder.

Christopher Dearden

Heaven's anger fell on Alfred Ball,
Who stole six apples from a stall.
The lightning flashed, the earth did quake,
And Alfred died – of tummy ache.

Sir Marcus Ordeyne

The Walrus

The Walrus lives on icy floes
And unsuspecting Eskimoes.

Don't bring your wife to Arctic Tundra
A Walrus may bob up from undra.

Michael Flanders

The Dog's Day

There are so many people who,
   While friendly to the dog,
Are distant to the kangaroo
   And cold towards the frog.

Anon.

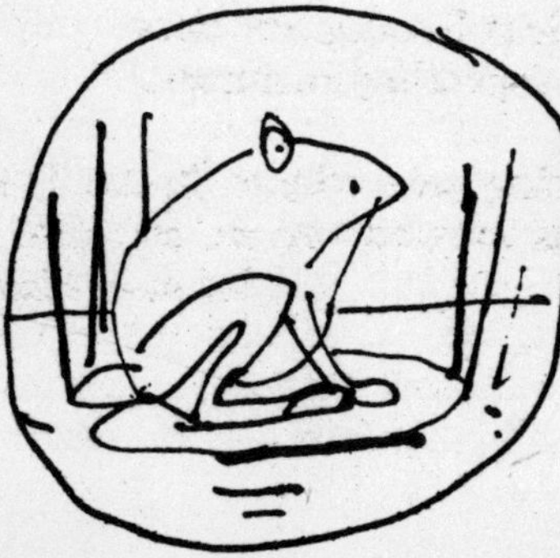

The Man with the Single Hair

He was not bald, for on his shining cranium
Remained one hair, its colour pink geranium.
Oh! How he idolized that single hair,
That, last of loved ones, grew luxuriant there.
He counted it each morning, fondly viewed it
This way, that way, carefully shampooed it,
Brushed it, combed it, scented it and oiled it,
Dared scarcely put his hat on, lest he soiled it.
In evening dress, arrayed for swell society,
He'd part it in the middle, for variety.
Oft-times he'd curl it, train it o'er his brow,
In careless fashion, as some bards do now,
Omitting nothing, with devoted care,
He'd pet his hirsute pride, his single hair.

But, sad to tell – ah bitter was the blow,
There came a day, a day of direst woe
When in his soup it fell!!! He quickly spied it,
Then rescued it, and on his napkin dried it,
His only hair! His pet! His flowing tress!
Chill was his forehead, deep his heart's distress.
'I'm bald, at last!' he wailed in bitter grief.
'My only hair has fallen like a leaf!

'What ho! A taxidermist!' shouted he.
'I'll have it stuffed, for all mankind to see.
And when within its case of glass installed,
The world shall see I was not always bald!'

Mel B. Spurr

Wild Flowers

'Of what are you afraid, my child?'
 inquired the kindly teacher.
'Oh, sir! the flowers, they are wild,'
 replied the timid creature.

Peter Newell

Mary had a crocodile
That ate a child a day;
But interfering people came
And took her pet away.
Sir Marcus Ordeyne

A Wise Old Owl

A wise old owl sat in an oak,
The more he heard, the less he spoke;
The less he spoke, the more he heard.
Why aren't we all like that wise old bird?

Anon.

Index of Poets

Allport, Herbert R. 78
Barr, Matthias 61
Bell, John Joy 27
Belloc, Hilaire 22
Bolt, T. 48
Braude, Michael 37, 65, 75
Chesterman, Hugh 39
Chesterton, G. K. 73
Cox, R. A. W. 24
Crawford, Tracey J. 47
Dearden, Christopher 84
Douglas, Lord Alfred 31
Eckersley, Roger 33, 55
Fear, Frank 41
Flanders, Michael 12, 86
Gibbons, David 53
Graham, Harry 17, 59
Griffin, Mike 14
Hoffenstein, Samuel 15, 38
Housman, A. E. 54
Husk, Nicholas
(Jonathan Curling) 28, 52
J. P. C. 83
Milligan, Spike 40, 51
Morton, J. B. 13
Nash, Ogden 19, 44
Newell, Peter 90
Ordeyne, Sir Marcus
26, 85, 91
Owen, Gareth 74
Parke, Walter 82
Reeves, James 34
Roberts, Paddy 32, 76
Rosen, Michael 36, 62
Sampson, Alistair 60, 68
Serraillier, Ian 71
Spurr, Mel B. 89
Taylor, Bert L. 80
Thackeray, W. M. 43
Trew, Cecil G. 70, 79
Upton, D. L. 64
Wells, Carolyn 56, 69
West, Colin 30, 77
Wilberforce, Samuel 67

Acknowledgements

The editor and publisher wish to thank the following for permission to use copyright material in this anthology:

Edward Arnold (Publishers) Ltd for 'Tender-Heartedness' and 'Waste', from *Ruthless Rhymes for Heartless Homes* by Harry Graham.

Associated Book Publishers Ltd for 'The Viking', from *Kings – And Other Things* by Hugh Chesterman.

B. T. Batsford Ltd for 'The Sword-Fish', from *Tails With a Twist* by Lord Alfred Douglas; © Edward Colman.

The Bodley Head for 'The Elephant', reprinted with permission of the Bodley Head from *The New Noah's Ark* by John Joy Bell.

Curtis Brown Ltd for 'The Lepidopterist' and 'A Caution to Hillbilly Singers, Harpists, Harpoonists, Channel-Swimmers, and People first in Line for World Series Tickets', from *The Private Dining Room* by Ogden Nash. Reprinted by permission of Curtis Brown Ltd, London, on behalf of the Estate of Ogden Nash. Also Little, Brown and Company for these two poems in Canada. 'The Lepidopterist', copyright 1952 by Ogden Nash, first appeared in *The New Yorker*, and 'A Caution to Hillbilly Singers . . . etc.', copyright 1950 by Ogden Nash, first appeared in *Cosmopolitan*. By permission of Little, Brown and Company.

Andre Deutsch Ltd for 'The Kite', 'The Jay' and 'Ungulates', from *Who's Zoo* by Michael Braude, 1963.

Andre Deutsch Ltd for 'Late last night' and 'Down behind the dustbin', from *Wouldn't You Like to Know* by Michael Rosen, 1977.

Dobson Books Ltd for 'The Duck-Billed Platypus' and 'The Walrus', from *Creatures Great and Small* by Michael Flanders (illustrations by Marcello Minale).

Dobson Books Ltd for 'The Darkest and Dingiest Dungeon', from *Out of the Blue from Nowhere*, and 'Putting the Shot', from *Back to Front and Back Again*, both by Colin West.

Gerald Duckworth Co. Ltd for 'The Hippopotamus', from *Cautionary Verses* by Hilaire Belloc.

David Gibbons for 'Mirror, mirror on the wall' by David Gibbons.

Liveright Publishing Corporation for 'Babies haven't any hair' and 'Twinkle, twinkle, little star', reprinted from *Poems in Praise of*

Practically Nothing by Samuel Hoffenstein, by permission of Liveright Publishing Corporation. Copyright 1928 by Samuel Hoffenstein. Copyright renewed 1955 by David Hoffenstein.

Spike Milligan Productions Ltd for 'Hello Jolly Guardsman' and 'You Must Never Bath in an Irish Stew', from *Silly Verse for Kids* by Spike Milligan (Puffin Books Ltd, 1968).

James Nisbet & Co. Ltd for 'Stay in your Seat', from *Hours of Sunshine* by Matthias Barr.

Oxford University Press for 'The Three Unlucky Men', from *The Blackbird in the Lilac* by James Reeves, 1952. Reprinted by permission of Oxford University Press.

Penguin Books Ltd for 'Unemployable' by Gareth Owen, from Gareth Owen, *Salford Road* (Kestrel Books, 1979) page 60; © 1971, 1974, 1976, 1979, Gareth Owen. Reprinted by permission of Penguin Books Ltd.

A. D. Peters & Co. Ltd for 'The Heron' by J. B. Morton from *Who's Who in the Zoo* (Eyre & Spottiswoode). Reprinted by permission of A. D. Peters & Co. Ltd.

Purnell Books for 'My Uncle and Aunt' and 'Mohair', first published by Sampson Low, Marston & Co. Ltd, 1946, in *Some Nonsense* by Roger Eckersley.

Routledge & Kegan Paul Ltd for 'In Days of Old' by R. A. W. Cox, from *Poems by Children*, edited by Michael Baldwin, London, 1962.

Alistair Sampson for 'The Gymnast' and 'There was once a Jill who loved her Jack till' by Alistair Sampson.

Ian Serraillier for 'The Headless Gardener'; © 1946 Ian Serraillier (from *Thomas and the Sparrow*, Oxford University Press).

The Society of Authors for 'Amelia mixed the mustard', as the literary representative of the Estate of A. E. Housman, and Jonathan Cape Ltd, publishers of A. E. Housman's *Collected Poems.*

Sweet & Maxwell Ltd for 'Lines to my Wig', from *Poetic Justice* by J. P. C., 1947.

Raphael Tuck & Sons Ltd for 'The Lizard' and 'Eggs', from *Bad Rhymes About Good Animals* by Cecil G. Trew, 1933.

D. L. Upton for 'Envelope' by D. L. Upton.

A. P. Watt Ltd for 'A Wish' by G. K. Chesterton. Reprinted with permission of Miss D. E. Collins.

The editor and publisher also wish to thank:

Harper & Row Publishers Inc. as the original publisher of 'Wild Flowers', from *Pictures and Rhymes* by Peter Newell.

The Bobbs-Merrill Co. Inc. as the original publisher of 'The Square Root' and 'A Lesson in Household Pets', from *Folly For the Wise* by Carolyn Wells.

The *Sunday Times* Magazine, and especially Sue Seddon and Sarah Spankie, for organizing the competition *It Could Be Verse*, and the following poets who were amongst the finalists: Tracey J. Crawford for 'The Bard at Bedtime', Christopher Dearden for 'Tight Squeeze', Frank Fear for 'If you should meet a Polar bear' and Mike Griffin for 'Oh To Be'.

If you've enjoyed this book,
Why not take a look
At *Not to be Taken Seriously*?
It will make you happy (deliriously).